# RICHARD O'BRIEN'S

# THE ROCKY HORROR SHOW

## VOCAL SELECTIONS

WISE PUBLICATIONS
LONDON/NEW YORK/SYDNEY

**Exclusive Distributors:**

Music Sales Limited
8/9 Frith Street, London W1V 5TZ, England.

Music Sales Pty Limited
120 Rothschild Avenue, Rosebery, NSW 2018, Australia.

This book © Copyright 1991
by Wise Publications
Order No.AM86101
ISBN 0.7119.2764.2

Book design by Icon Design Solutions

Music Sales' complete catalogue lists thousands of titles and is free from your local music shop,
or direct from Music Sales Limited.
Please send a cheque/postal order for£1.50 for postage to: Music Sales Limited,
Newmarket Road, Bury St. Edmunds, Suffolk IP33 3YB.

Printed in the United Kingdom by
J.B. Offset Printers (Marks Tey) Limited, Marks Tey, Essex.

**SCIENCE FICTION - DOUBLE FEATURE** 9

**DAMN IT, JANET** 12

**OVER AT THE FRANKENSTEIN PLACE** 16

**THE TIME WARP** 19

**SWEET TRANSVESTITE** 25

**THE SWORD OF DAMOCLES** 30

**I CAN MAKE YOU A MAN** 34

**HOT PATOOTIE - BLESS MY SOUL** 36

**I CAN MAKE YOU A MAN: REPRISE** 40

**TOUCH-A TOUCH-A TOUCH-A TOUCH ME** 42

**ONCE IN A WHILE** 46

**EDDIE'S TEDDY** 49

**PLANET SCHMANET** 54

**FLOOR SHOW** 58

**(A) ROSE TINT MY WORLD**

**(B) DON'T DREAM IT**

**(C) WILD AND UNTAMED THING**

**I'M GOING HOME** 66

**SUPER HEROES** 68

**SCIENCE FICTION/DOUBLE FEATURE: REPRISE** 70

# SCIENCE FICTION - DOUBLE FEATURE

CUE:- "Glad you could come tonight."

caught in a cel - lu - loid jam___ Then at a dead - ly pace_ it came from
pass-ing them used lots of skills___ And when worlds col - lide_ said George

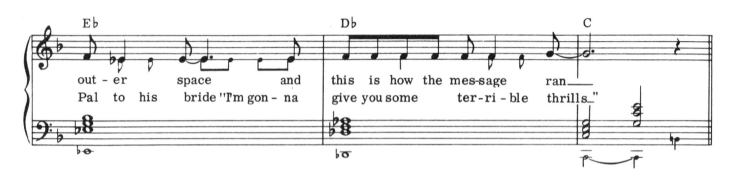

out - er space and this is how the mes-sage ran___
Pal to his bride "I'm gon - na give you some ter - ri - ble thrills"

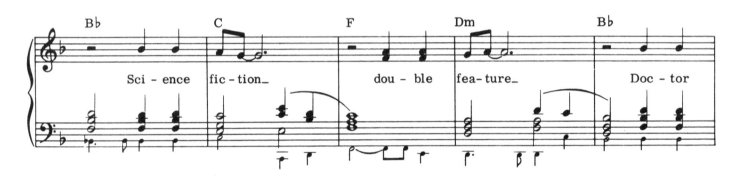

Sci - ence fic -tion_ dou - ble fea-ture_ Doc - tor

X___ will build a crea-ture See An - droids fight-ing_

Brad and Jan-et___ Anne Fran-cis stars in___ "For- bid -den

# DAMN IT, JANET

CUE:- "And Ralph himself will be in line for promotion in a year or two"    *(Janet Sits)*

(Brad) *(Spoken)*    *mf*    Hey Janet, I got something to say I really loved the skillful way    *(Sung)* You

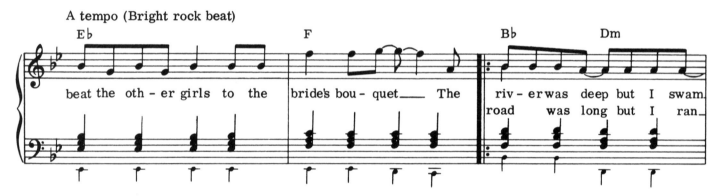

beat the oth - er girls to the bride's bou - quet__ The

riv - er was deep but I swam__
road was long but I ran

__ it, (Jan - et) The fu - ture is ours__ so let's plan __ it, (Jan - et) So
__ it, (Jan - et) There's a fire in my heart and you fan __ it, (Jan - et) If there's

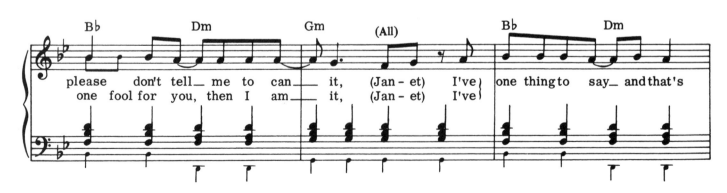

please don't tell__ me to can __ it, (Jan - et) I've) one thing to say__ and that's
one fool for you, then I am __ it, (Jan - et) I've)

damn it Jan-et     I love you_____     The

Here's a ring to prove that I'm no jok-er_____

There's three ways that love_____ can grow_____

That's good bad or me-di-o-cre_____ Oh

Jan-et_____ I love you so_____ (Janet) Oh it's

**D.S. al Coda**

**CODA**

*molto rit.*

# OVER AT THE FRANKENSTEIN PLACE

CUE: "Besides, darling, the owner of the phone may be a beautiful
woman, and you may never come back"

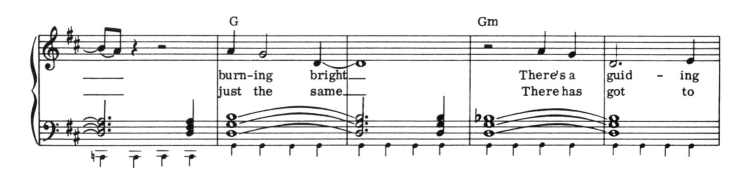

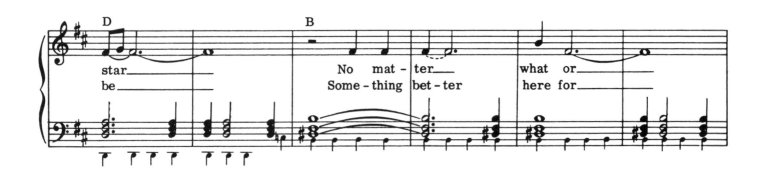

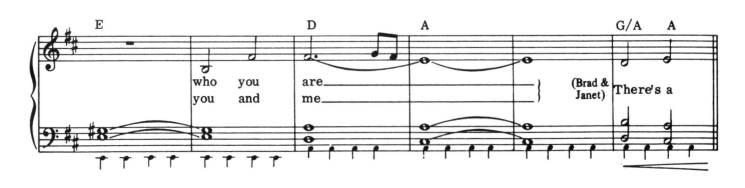

of night's dream-ing___ Flow mor-phia

slow let the sun___ and light come stream-ing

in-to my life___

___ In-to my life___

*crescendo poco a poco*

***D.S. al Coda***

(Brad & Janet) There's a

**CODA**

(Brad & Janet) in the

dark-ness___ of ev-'ry - - bod-y's life.___

*molto rit.*

# THE TIME WARP

CUE:- "It seemed like only yesterday since he went"
"Where?"
"To pieces!"

gain.

(Columbia) Well I was tap-ping down the street just-a hav-ing a think, When a snake of a guy gave me an e-vil wink, We-ell it shook me up, it took me by sur-prise, He had a pick up truck and the de-vil's eyes He stared at me and I felt a change Time meant noth-ing, nev-er would a-gain

(All) Let's do the Time Warp a-gain

Let's do the Time Warp a-gain

# SWEET TRANSVESTITE

CUE: "Master!"

night I am one hell of a lov -er___ I'm just a sweet trans -ves -tite___

from Tran sex -ual Tran - syl -van -i - a

a - a___ Let me show you a - round, may -be

play you a sound you look like you're both pret - ty groo -vy___ But if you

want some - thing vis - ual that's not too a - bys - mal we could

take in an old Steve Reeves mo - vie_(Brad) I'm glad we caught you at home, Could we

*(Spoken)*

26

from Tran - sex - ual Tran - syl - van - i - a - -

a - a - Why don't you stay for the night or

may - be a bite I could show you my fav - 'rite ob - ses -

- sion I've been mak-ing a man with blonde hair and a tan and he's

good for re - liev - ing my ten - sion I'm just a

sweet trans - ves - tite from Tran - sex - ual

28

# THE SWORD OF DAMOCLES

CUE:- "Throw open the switches on the Sonic oscillator and
step up the reactor power input three more points"
(ROCKY is unbandaged by FRANK)

# I CAN MAKE YOU A MAN

CUE: - FRANK! "I didn't make him for you" . . . . . . . . . *(Wait for Nod)*

# HOT PATOOTIE - BLESS MY SOUL

CUE:- COLUMBIA:- "Eddie!" (as she opens 'fridge)
EDDIE:- 1. 2. 3.

(Chorus) Hot Pa-too-tie bless my soul___ I real-ly love that rock and roll

G               A             C           G

(Eddie) Hot Pa-too-tie bless my soul___ I real-ly love that rock and roll___

(Janet) Hot Pa - too - tie___ bless my

(Chorus) Hot Pa-too-tie bless my soul___ I real-ly love that

G               A             C

(Eddie) Hot Pa - too - tie bless my soul___ I real-ly love that

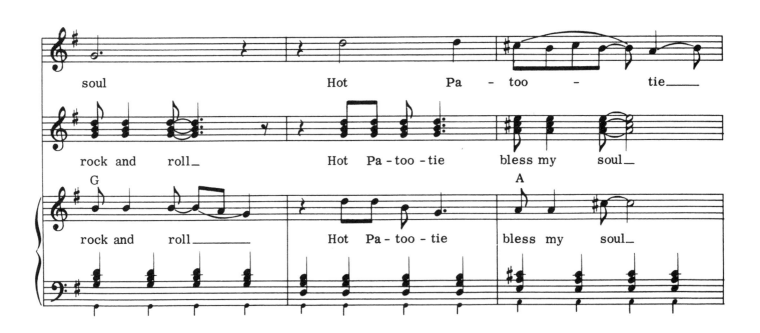

soul                 Hot Pa - too - tie___

rock and roll___ Hot Pa-too-tie bless my soul___

G                                     A

rock and roll___ Hot Pa - too - tie bless my soul___

**⊕ CODA**

# I CAN MAKE YOU A MAN: REPRISE

CUE:- FRANK! "We had a mental relationship"

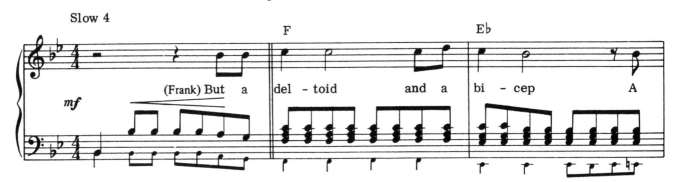

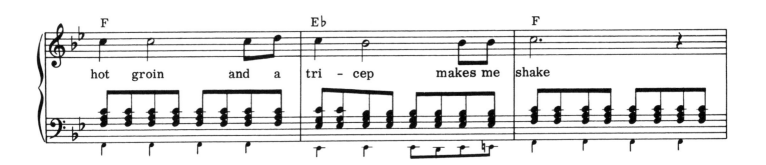

# TOUCH-A TOUCH-A TOUCH-A TOUCH ME

CUE:- NARRATOR:- "There seemed little doubt that she was indeed his slave"

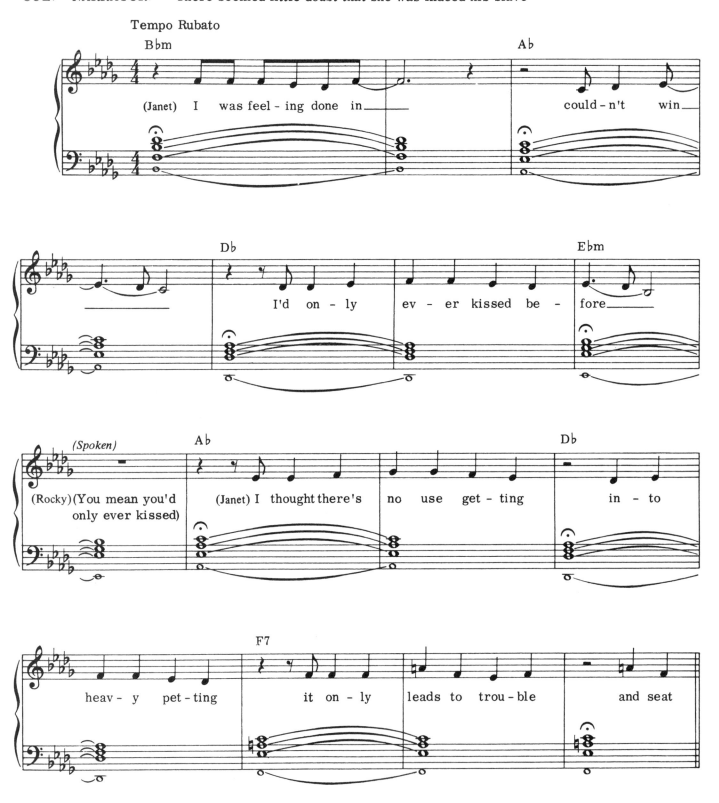

# ONCE IN A WHILE

CUE:- NARRATOR:- "And Brad, you may be sure, had plenty of heart.

(Janet sings harmony)

and phone my place, it-'ll be O. K. And that's all the time

that it ta - - - kes

for a heart to beat a - gain So give me a sign

that a lov-er ma - - kes You look a - round

the one you've found is back a - gain.

# EDDIE'S TEDDY

CUE:- BRAD "Tell 'em Doc"

me in a note which reads_ "I'm out of my head_ (Narrator) Oh hur-ry or I may be dead_ (Dr. Scott) They must-n't car-ry out their ev-il deeds" When Ed-die said he did-n't like his ted-dy you knew he was a no good kid_ But when he threat-ened your life_ with a switch blade knife, what a guy, makes you cry,_ and I

(All)

(Frank) (Janet) (Dr. Scott)

# PLANET SCHMANET

CUE:- FRANK:- "O.K. it's Startime."

don't taste too nice You'd bet-ter wise

—— up Jan-et Weiss——

I've laid the seed—— it should be all—— you need

You're as sen-sual as a pen-cil, wound up like an E or first string

When we made it did ya hear a bell ring You got a

57

# FLOOR SHOW

(a) Rose Tint My World
(b) Don't Dream It
(c) Wild And Untamed Thing

CUE:- NARRATOR:- "it was clear that this was to be no picnic!"

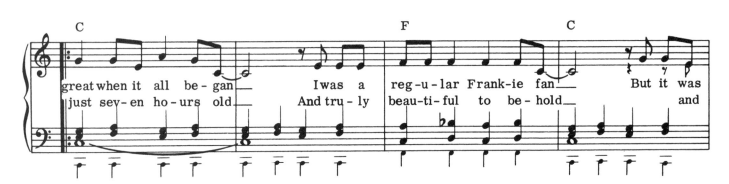

It's be- yond me, help me mom- my God bless Li- ly St. Cyr.
(Brad)
(Janet)

Fast rock

(Frank) My my my my my my my my __ My my my my my _____ I'm a

wild and an un- tamed thing ___ I'm a bee with a dead- ly sting ___

Get a hit and your mind goes ping _____ your heart 'll

thump and your blood will sing ___ So let the par- ty and the sounds rock on ___

I'm gon- na shake it till the life has gone ___ Rose tint my world, keep me

safe from my trou-ble and pain

We're a

wild and an un-tamed thing ___ we're a bee with a dead-ly sting

Get a hit and your mind goes ping ___ your heart 'll

thump and your blood will sing ___ So let the par-ty and the sounds rock on ___

We're gon-na shake it till the life has gone ___ Rose tint our world keep us

safe from our trou - ble and pain ____ We're a ____

Frank n' Fur - ter it's all o - ver, your
(Riff Raff)

mis - sion is a fail - ure, your life style's too ex - treme ____

I'm your new com - man - der you now are my pris - on - er We re-
*(Spoken)*

-turn to Tran - syl - van - ia Pre - pare the tran - sit beam.
*(Sung)*

# I'M GOING HOME

CUE:- "Wait, I can explain"

# SUPER HEROES

CUE:- RIFF RAFF "Activate the transit crystal"

And all I know____ is still the beast is feed-ing____

Ah____ Ah____

Ah____ Ah____

Ah____ Ah____

(Narrator)
(Spoken) And crawling on the planets face some insects called the human race

lost in time and lost in space and mean - ing (Sung) mean - ing.____

# SCIENCE FICTION/DOUBLE FEATURE: REPRISE

CUE:- NARRATOR exits, USHERETTE appears.

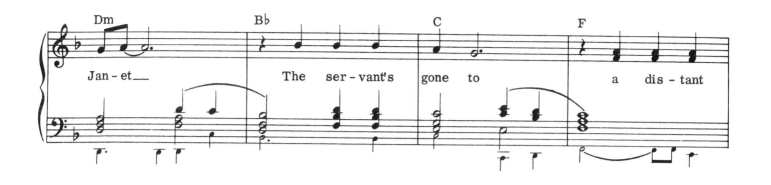

Jan-et___ The ser-vant's gone to a dis-tant

plan-et Oh oh oh oh___ To the late night dou-ble

fea-ture pic-ture show___ I wan-na go___ Oh oh___

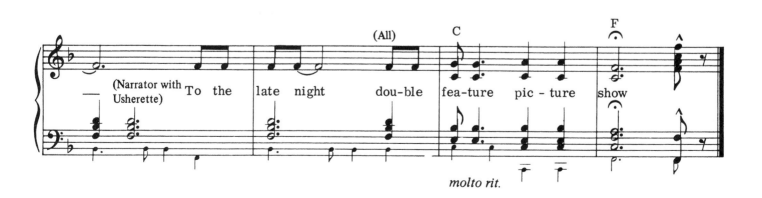

(Narrator with Usherette) (All) To the late night dou-ble fea-ture pic-ture show

*molto rit.*